ADORATION OF THE OLD WOMAN

José Rivera

BROADWAY PLAY PUBLISHING INC
New York
www.broadwayplaypublishing.com
info@broadwayplaypublishing.com

ADORATION OF THE OLD WOMAN
© Copyright 2010 by José Rivera

First printing: November 2010
Second printing: September 2011
I S B N: 978-0-88145-430-7

Book design: Marie Donovan
Typographic controls & page make-up: Adobe InDesign
Typeface: Palatino
Printed and bound in the U S A

ABOUT THE AUTHOR

José Rivera is a recipient of two OBIE Awards for
Playwriting (for MARISOL and REFERENCES TO
SALVADOR DALI MAKE ME HOT, both at The
Joseph Papp Public Theater), a Fulbright Arts
Fellowship, a Whiting Foundation Award, a McKnight
Fellowship, and a 2005 Impact Award. He studied
with Gabriel García Márquez at Sundance and was
writer-in-residence at the Royal Court Theater,
London.

U S theater productions include THE HOUSE
OF RAMON IGLESIA (Ensemble Studio Theater,
American Playhouse), MARISOL (Humana Festival,
La Jolla Playhouse, Hartford Stage Co), CLOUD
TECTONICS (Humana Festival, Playwrights Horizons,
Goodman Theater), REFERENCES TO SALVADOR
DALI MAKE ME HOT (South Coast Rep), EACH
DAY DIES WITH SLEEP (Circle Rep, Berkeley Rep),
SONNETS FOR AN OLD CENTURY (Greenway Arts
Alliance), SUEÑO (Hartford Stage, Manhattan Class
Company, Milwaukee Rep), GIANTS HAVE US IN
THEIR BOOKS (Magic Theater, INTAR Theater),
MARICELA DE LA LUZ LIGHTS THE WORLD (La
Jolla Playhouse), THE PROMISE (Ensemble Studio
Theater, Los Angeles Theater Center), THE STREET
OF THE SUN (Mark Taper Forum), ADORATION OF
THE OLD WOMAN (La Jolla Playhouse), SCHOOL
OF THE AMERICAS (Joseph Papp Public Theater and

LAByrinth Theater), MASSACRE (SING TO YOUR CHILDREN) (Goodman Theater and Teatro Vista), BRAINPEOPLE (A C T, San Francisco), BOLEROS FOR THE DISENCHANTED (Yale Rep, Huntington Stage, A C T, Goodman Theater), YELLOW (Collaboraction), and HUMAN EMOTIONAL PROCESS (commission at the McCarter Theater). His work has been seen in Puerto Rico, London, Paris, Edinburgh, Mexico City, Singapore, Greece, Sweden, Norway, Canada, Peru, Australia, Germany, Romania, and the Philippines.

The screenplay for his first produced film *The Motorcycle Diaries* (Walter Salles, director) was nominated for a 2005 Academy Award for Best Adapted Screenplay, a BAFTA Award, and a Writers Guild Award, and received Spain's Goya Award for Best Adapted Screenplay as well as Argentina's top screenwriting award. For television he co-created and produced the series *Eerie, Indiana* (N B C). In 2006 he wrote and directed the short film *The Tape Recorder* (with Sona Tatoyan). His film *Trade* (Lionsgate Pictures) premiered at the 2007 Sundance Film Festival and was the first film to premiere at the United Nations. He has written screen adaptations of Kerouac's *On The Road* (Francis Ford Coppola, producer, Walter Salles, director), *Three Apples Fell From Heaven* (Door/Key Productions), and the novel *The Brief Wondrous Life of Oscar Wao* (Walter Salles, director). *Celestina*, a film based on CLOUD TECTONICS, will mark his debut as a feature film director.

Rivera serves on the board of PEN West, and is a member of The LAByrinth Theater Company.

ADORATION OF THE OLD WOMAN was commissioned by the La Jolla Playhouse and developed with the assistance of the Ensemble Studio Theatre West Playwrights Unit, the Mark Taper Forum Mentor Playwrights, the Sundance Theatre Laboratory, and the Joseph Papp Public Theater.

Many thanks to Camilia Monet, Javi Mulero, Ana Ortiz, Alexis Cruz, Ivonne Coll, Elizabeth Logun, Jo Bonney, Robert Blacker, George C Wolfe, Phillip Himberg, Priscilla Lopez, Sona Tatoyan, Carlo Alban, Onahoua Rodriguez, the National Endowment for the Arts, and the James Irvine Foundation.

ADORATION OF THE OLD WOMAN opened at the La Jolla Playhouse (Des McAnuff, Artistic Director; Terence Dwyer, Managing Director; Shirley Fishman, Associate Artistic Director) on 17 September 2002. The cast and creative contributors were:

ADORACIÓN	Marisol Padilla Sanchez
DOÑA BELEN	Ivonne Coll
VANESSA	Tamara Mello
ISMAEL	Gary Perez
CHEO	John Ortiz

Director	Jo Bonney
Scenic design	Neil Patel
Costume design	Emilio Sosa
Lighting design	Chris Akerlind
Sound design	Darron West
Dramaturg	Shirley Fishman
Fight director	Steve Rankin
Stage manager	Diana Moser

CHARACTERS & SETTING

ADORACIÓN
DOÑA BELEN
VANESSA
ISMAEL
CHEO

Time: Later this year

Place: Las Arenas, Puerto Rico

ACT ONE

Scene One. Early morning, January 6. DOÑA BELEN's house.
Scene Two. That evening. Same.
Scene Three. Later that night. Same.

ACT TWO

Scene One. A month later, day. Same.
Scene Two. That night. Same.
Scene Three. Later, the next morning. Same.
Scene Four. A few days later, day. Same.
Scene Five. The next night. Same.
Scene Six. Three days later, day. Same.

The night is an immense star of emotion and in her I
sleep the dream that lays me in your soul.
Julia de Burgos

The countries the United States have taken in trust,
Puerto Rico and the Philippines, must first accept the
discipline of law. They are children and we are men in
these deep matters of government and justice.
Woodrow Wilson

History is wrong and always has to be rewritten.
George Santayana

for Adena and Teo

ACT ONE

Scene 1

(*Early morning, January 6.*)

(*A one-bedroom concrete house in rural, near-future Puerto Rico.*)

(*A porch with a rocking chair. Living room. Bedroom. All brightly painted, adorned with religious artifacts, but run-down, some mold on the walls.*)

(*A mattress set on a wooden palette, raised off the ground by bricks: BELEN's bed. An elaborately carved headboard decorated with Santos, Madonnas, stuffed white birds, crosses, the hair of dead children.*)

(*A machete leans against the wall.*)

(*A door to the offstage bathroom.*)

(*Two women lie in bed—ancient DOÑA BELEN and young, beautiful ADORACIÓN—mid-conversation:*)

ADORACIÓN: It's true! Nobody's got an education in Las Arenas, but you don't really need one when rumors are ripe and sweet—

BELEN: (*Praying*) Mary, dear Mary, apocalyptic Mother of—

ADORACIÓN: And the new ones are delicious! Rumors of war, independence, forests full of *guerrilleros*, caves full of machetes—

BELEN: *(Praying)* Virgin womb, divine seed-carrier, blessed tit that suckled our Savior!

ADORACIÓN: Listen to me, old woman, you'll learn something.

BELEN: *(Praying)* Holy nipples, full of grace, hard, sweet, may the thirsty tongue of Christ lick you day and—

ADORACIÓN: Ay, slow down there, lady!

BELEN: *(Praying)* Creative Mother of divine light, take away the darkness hovering over my bed—

ADORACIÓN: *(Getting closer to* BELEN*)* Do you believe the rumors or not? If the people vote for independence and the gringos say no, will a war really come? God! There's no way the gringos will beat Puerto Rico this time! *(Whispers)* There are too many soldiers, you know, buried below us. Patriots who died without firing a shot or raising a machete in anger. Their blood stains the clay and enriches the trees. They are the army of our liberation, all the proud dead, you'll see.

(BELEN *pushes* ADORACIÓN.)

BELEN: Move over.

ADORACIÓN: You move over. Fat cow. Ugly fat cow ass.

(ADORACIÓN *slaps* BELEN *on the ass.*)

BELEN: *(Praying)* If Christ Jesus can endure hours of torture on the Tree of Suffering, I can too!

ADORACIÓN: You know all about rumors. I've seen your fat ass swing from house to house like an *aguacate* tree in a hurricane, advertising God-knows-what, gossiping, telling your lies.

BELEN: I don't lie. You do. You can't breathe without lying. And you're a whore too. Whore!

ADORACIÓN: *(Laughing)* Is "whore" the best you can—?

BELEN: Bitch!

ADORACIÓN: Oooooo stop.

BELEN: Marriage-destroying, scheming, two-faced, dog-licking slut-bitch!

ADORACIÓN: *(Laughing)* Yes, alright.

BELEN: You can go to Hell and burn in Hell and leave me alone.

ADORACIÓN: Ay, dear Doña Belen, you should watch what you say because you don't know what you're talking about. I know about Hell. I've *seen* it. When I say Hell I know what I'm—

BELEN: You've seen it all. Have you seen my cunt?

ADORACIÓN: You talk about Hell but you might as well be talking about Ponce or Mayagüez because you've never seen those places, you don't know what they're like, and you don't know Hell.

BELEN: Smell my cunt.

ADORACIÓN: I can't believe you talk about that thing so much. Like it's something I even want to imagine.

BELEN: You don't have to imagine. I'll show it to you. It looks like this. *(She makes a face, imitating her cunt.)*

ADORACIÓN: Beautiful. Makes me wish I were a man, like Don Toli, with a thick, lovely tree between my legs.

BELEN: My cunt looks like the opening to Hell. Now, shut up and let me sleep. *(She closes her eyes and tries to sleep.)*

(After a moment, ADORACIÓN puts her arms around BELEN.)

ADORACIÓN: I'll tell you why *campesinos* have so many rumors. When you don't have money, you have words. *Information* is what keeps a little barrio like this, so poor and isolated, feeling alive. But rumors go bad. They get mixed with lies and travel like a virus through the guts of the town, making everyone sick, and no *bruja* can stop it.

(BELEN *looks into* ADORACIÓN's *eyes, as if she's trying to read the past.*)

BELEN: Is that what killed you? The rumors?

ADORACIÓN: Your ugly words did it, as if you didn't know!

BELEN: Well, it should've been a knife, *carajo*!

ADORACIÓN: Ay, you have an ugly mind!

BELEN: I should've opened your chest with Toli's machete. Yanked your heart out of this corrupted body—this dry, meatless rag—how any man could stick it into this smelly, little hole—

ADORACIÓN: Stop it right now—!

BELEN: This is my bed. Toli made this bed for me. I slept here. Loved here. Had seven miscarriages here. I do an old woman's lonely work and I collapse here every night. You don't tell me what to do in my bed!

ADORACIÓN: Yeah? Well, while you were at church, telling God your lies, your husband, your dear Don Toli, and I were in this bed, fucking like dogs.

BELEN: *(Crying)* ...no more, stop...

(ADORACIÓN *laughs, stretches out luxuriously.*)

ADORACIÓN: God gives us a body to use. A voice to scream it. Legs to encircle. Hips to bear the weight. All the while...you expand, you inflate, to fill the world with your joy. I was breakfast, lunch, and dinner for that poor, hungry man. I never ran out—

(*A knock on* BELEN'*s door interrupts them. The women look at each other, apprehensive.*)

(BELEN *gets out of bed and shuffles to the living room.*)

(ADORACIÓN *waits and listens.*)

(*In the living room,* BELEN *opens the door.*)

(VANESSA *is there, surrounded by suitcases.* VANESSA *is seventeen, dressed in dark urban clothes, heavy boots, completely wrong for the tropical sun, sunglasses, bandana, low-cut jeans.*)

(*Though we hear English,* BELEN *is speaking Spanish,* VANESSA *is speaking English and neither can understand the other.*)

(*The women look at each other a long moment.*)

VANESSA: Great-grandmother?

BELEN: Who the hell are you?

VANESSA: It's me Vanessa.

BELEN: (*Trying to be pleasant*) Whatever you're selling, girl, tell K-Mart I don't want it.

VANESSA: Vanessa. My name. Vanessa. Va-ne-ssa!

BELEN: Yes, yes, Va-ne-ssa, for the love of—

VANESSA: Vanessa from Paterson—my mom wrote to you. My parents are *Florencia and Enrique Aponte*?

BELEN: Who the fuck are they?

VANESSA: (*Reading a scrap of paper*) Are you Doña Belen Berdecia?

BELEN: I am Doña Belen Berdecia Aleida.

VANESSA: (*Showing* BELEN *the paper*) Are we in Las Arenas?

BELEN: (*Can't read*) What's wrong with this idiot child?

VANESSA: Mami wrote you letters 'cause you have no phone....

(VANESSA *takes out a cell-phone, punches a number.)*

BELEN: If you're a Mormon you can take the warmed-over Jesus you bought at K-Mart and shove it up the ass of your gringo bosses.

VANESSA: *(On the phone)* Mami? Vanessa.

BELEN: *(Re: the telephone)* What the hell is that?

VANESSA: *(On the phone)* I'm standing right in front of her. She looks like she wants to hit me. And she's old. And her house is a shack. Here.

(VANESSA *holds the phone out to* BELEN.)

BELEN: Don't put that thing in my—

VANESSA: Tel-e-phone.

BELEN: Ay, it's a telephone. Where the hell's the wire? God Almighty. The gringos have done away with civilization at last. They can talk to the air!

VANESSA: *(Into the phone)* The town that time forgot, yo!

(BELEN *takes the phone.)*

BELEN: *(On the phone)* What? *(Beat)* Yes. *(Beat)* You're *Celia's* daughter? *My* Celia? Ay, my dear granddaughter! Ay, Florencia, the last time I saw you, there was shit running down your leg and I chased you half way to Jerusalem before you let me change your diaper, may God bless you and keep you in the Glorious Light of Jesus the— *(Beat)* Yes. *(Beat)* Yes.

(VANESSA *finds three unopened letters from her parents on* BELEN's *table.)*

VANESSA: You're supposed to *read* your mail. *(Grabs the phone)* This is horseshit, if you think this is good for me, you're outta your—shut it, Mami—I'm gonna find drugs, and do them, and shoplift, and jump an

unemployed slacker Puerto Rican, have his bastard
baby, and you're gonna look like the biggest asshole in
the—

(Her mother hangs up.)

(VANESSA turns the phone off.)

(BELEN looks at VANESSA, tears in her eyes.)

BELEN: Look at you, *bendito*, so full of sweetness and
love, my dear great-granddaughter...

*(BELEN embraces VANESSA and covers her face in kisses. She
makes the sign of the cross over VANESSA's face and chest.)*

VANESSA: *(Pulling away)* Quit that.

BELEN: I see Toli in your eyes, Celia in those lips,
the soul of my seven unborn babies, taken from this
ungrateful shit-world too soon, swept from the floor of
the world by God before I got a chance to mourn them.
Sit, sit, oh God you're too skinny, just a rag, I have
some chocolate and cigarettes.

VANESSA: *(To the universe)* This is my *tomb* right here.

BELEN: I see the Puerto Rican in you...though you've
done everything in your power to disguise it, those
gringo clothes, vulgar shoes—you don't smell like any
woman I've ever smelled: yet you *are* Boricua. They
can keep you prisoner a hundred years, the Boricua
will always show. I see it as I see it in myself. It's the
beautiful thing you hide from the world.

*(Desperate to communicate, VANESSA takes out a Spanish/
English phrase book.)*

*(Italics in dialogue indicate characters have switched to their
second language.)*

*(VANESSA's second language is a labored and heavily-
accented Spanish.)*

(BELEN's *second language is a heavily-accented and halting English.*)

VANESSA: *I. Am. Vanessa.*

BELEN: *(Shaking her head)* Ay, it's a sin how they've corrupted you. You lost your humanity because you're Looking Out for Number One. That's what they do up in Paterson—

VANESSA: Paterson!

BELEN: They take our little flowers—the bloom and glory of His Imagination, the pride of our culture—and shit all over them.

VANESSA: *(Reading from book) I am well. How are you?*

BELEN: I'm fine, thank you, how are you?

VANESSA: *Do you have? A room for bathing?*

BELEN: Do I have a what?

VANESSA: Jesus, that's all I know, it's not like they bothered to teach me Spanish! Oh, Mami's a blond now! She goes by Flo, nobody calls her Florencia. She's being so white it's not even—

BELEN: Don't you know a single word?

VANESSA: Don't you know a single word?

BELEN: Ay, what have they done to your language?

VANESSA: *Bathroom?*

BELEN: *Good morning, Teacher.*

VANESSA: Good morning, Teacher? *(Laughs)* That's so good. Good morning, Teacher.

BELEN: *Good morning, Teacher!*

VANESSA: Lookit, I'm gonna find el BATHROOM, before I URINATE on el floor. *(She squats, pantomiming going to the bathroom.)*

BELEN: *(Shocked, pointing off)* The bathroom's through there, child, don't be stupid.

(VANESSA crosses to BELEN's bedroom on the way to the bathroom.)

(ADORACIÓN sees VANESSA.)

(VANESSA pauses in the bedroom, senses something—then exits to the offstage bathroom.)

(When she's alone, BELEN often talks to herself, having imaginary conversations with people who aren't there.)

(BELEN now "talks" to VANESSA's mother, Florencia.)

BELEN: Of course, I'll take your daughter in, she's blood after all. I know it's popular with the gringos to deny blood and let your family die in the streets covered in snow, even on Three Kings Day, but that's not how things are done down here!

VANESSA: *(Off)* Your bathroom is disgusting!

(BELEN thinks about VANESSA, speaks as if VANESSA were in the room.)

BELEN: You're very angry, aren't you child? The anger comes from having a hole in your body and I don't mean the little one between your legs. I mean the one in your heart. It's the hole normally filled by God and most of the Popes. You tried to fill that hole with things. Shoes, lipstick—sex—yes, sex—because I have serious doubts about your virginity, girl. Those things don't fill the hole. They go in and fall forever, because the hole of God in the human body is infinite, can't be filled by K-Mart. The body knows this and feels cheated. So there's anger. Storms and waterfalls of anger. You're consumed by it, little angel.

ISMAEL: *(Off)* Where's the queen of the house? The queen of my affections?

(ISMAEL *enters. He is a large man, thirty, powerfully built, with fat, soft hands. He brings a chainsaw.*)

BELEN: Ay, Ismael, come in, my dear son—you brought it?

(ISMAEL *holds up the chainsaw.*)

ISMAEL: The exorcist.

BELEN: *(Excited, to* ISMAEL*)* May the Heavenly Saints protect you from the violence of the Coming Apocalypse!

ISMAEL: Thank you and I hope you're right. The only blood I want to see on Judgement Day is the blood of animals and the Castro brothers.

BELEN: Ah, but in the end, my beloved, animals too will enjoy the blissful reunion with the Heavenly Architect. As for the Commies, fuck 'em...

ISMAEL: *(Skeptical)* Animals are going to Heaven?

BELEN: Yes! All living things—

ISMAEL: Scorpions and tarantulas too?

BELEN: Well...maybe not scorpions and taran...

ISMAEL: What about mosquitoes?

BELEN: No, mosquitoes will be exempt from the Glorious Explosion of Peace, now that I think—

ISMAEL: Cockroaches? Centipedes?

(VANESSA *re-enters, zipping her fly.*)

BELEN: Ismael, meet my great-granddaughter from North America, Paterson. Inside that angry face and those barbaric clothes is a beautiful Boricua flower.

ISMAEL: *(Holding out his hand)* It's a pleasure to meet you. Welcome to our enchanted island. Pearl of the Caribbean. My name is Ismael.

VANESSA: *(With no hope, to* ISMAEL*)* Do you speak any English?

*(*ISMAEL *switches to his second language, a fluent, slightly accented English.)*

ISMAEL: *I do, young lady.*

VANESSA: Thank God!

ISMAEL: *(Good-natured laugh) Doña Belen's English is limited.*

VANESSA: To "good morning, Teacher!"

BELEN: *Good morning, Teacher!*

ISMAEL: *Are you on vacation?*

VANESSA: Vacation? Try total, degrading *exile.*

ISMAEL: *(Laughs) You speak English at the university level.*

BELEN: *(To* ISMAEL*)* Isn't she beautiful? She'd make a challenging wife, Ismael.

ISMAEL: *(Proud, to* VANESSA*) Do you know your great-grandmother is between a hundred and a hundred and fifty years old? Some say she was born the year of our liberation from Spain, 1898, a treasure of this barrio. But no one knows for sure.*

BELEN: *(Impatient)* Ay, tell her about the bed! About the depth of my suffering. How the moon looks down on me and laughs!

ISMAEL: *(Holds her) Bendito,* poor, sainted Doña...

BELEN: If I knew how to write, I'd send the Pope a letter and he'd understand. Only you understand. May the Holy Spirit fold his wings around the armor of your heavy heart and burn away your sorrows.

ISMAEL: *(To* VANESSA*) Her bed is haunted. Every night the ghost of Adoración Celia Lomar lies next to her...whispers in Doña's ear her lies and pornography, making the old woman go crazy. No photos exist, but they say Adoración was the* *most beautiful girl in Las Arenas—don't tell La Doña I said that! She was poor, religious, her father beat her for being independent. They say she used to yell at the American foremen in the cane fields, in English: "Why you no give them water? Why you no pay more money?" (Beat, sotto) But she was best known for being Don Toli's mistress.*

BELEN: I was beautiful. I had a figure like a violin.

(As BELEN tells VANESSA this story, ISMAEL whispers a simultaneous English translation into VANESSA's ear.)

ISMAEL: *(Sotto to VANESSA) I had a figure like a violin...*

BELEN: You could tell by my hips I would bear a hundred powerful children. I couldn't read but I knew everything there was to know about men and women. I had a sense of humor. I could sing. I could carry my own weight in barrels of water and bundles of sugarcane. I could slaughter pigs. I could love all night. And men are so stupid, they have the very best, yet they're never satisfied. They sniff the air. "Ah, I smell some available pussy over there." How much more pussy does a man need, I ask you! Toli had a Caribbean queen. But it wasn't enough for him. He wanted the Mulatta Whore of Las Arenas. It was my destiny to love a man other women adored. I could have picked an ugly man, a monkey who smelled like piss. No. My man smelled like honey. Well, nobody takes what's mine! I had sixteen brothers and sisters and if I wanted a drink of water or a cup of rice I fought them all like a savage and I got what was mine—even with hookworms eating my guts!

ISMAEL: *(Sotto to VANESSA) ...even with hookworms eating my guts.*

VANESSA: Whoa.

(BELEN impatiently pushes VANESSA and ISMAEL toward her bedroom. He whispers to VANESSA.)

ISMAEL: *(Entering room, to* VANESSA*) Rumor is—
Adoración died in childbirth. Having Toli's baby.*

VANESSA: Whoa *again.*

(In the bedroom, ISMAEL *and* VANESSA *do not see*
ADORACIÓN.*)*

*(*VANESSA *admires the beautiful bed.)*

*(*ADORACIÓN*'s eyes are fixed on* VANESSA.*)*

ISMAEL: *Doña killed half the chickens in the barrio trying to
get rid of the ghost—nothing. Now she goes from house to
house, looking for someone to cut the bed in half. She wants
me to take the haunted half to the woods to burn it.*

BELEN: *(Blessing the chainsaw)* May God bless the
sparking plugs and iron teeth of this chainsaw, amen.

ISMAEL: Amen. *(He eyes the headboard and pulls the chord
on the chainsaw. Nothing happens. He pulls repeatedly—
nothing.)* I don't know what's—

BELEN: God, no. Not another—

ISMAEL: It was working this morn—

BELEN: The whore's put a spell on it!

ISMAEL: *(Checking the chainsaw)* I don't get it—

BELEN: *(To* ISMAEL*)* Get out! Go! Take that piece of shit
with you! Imbecile! Loser!

ADORACIÓN: *(To* BELEN, *re* VANESSA*)* I know her eyes,
Belen...!

BELEN: *(To* ADORACIÓN*)* I swear by the mother that
bore you, if I catch you looking at her, I'll... *(To* ISMAEL
and VANESSA.*)* What are you looking at? Get out!

*(*BELEN *tries to give* ISMAEL *a cocotaso.)*

*(*ISMAEL *and* VANESSA *rush out of the room.)*

*(*BELEN *collapses on the bed.)*

VANESSA: What just happened?

ISMAEL: *You stay long enough you'll learn the whole island's full of ghosts. And they all want a piece of you.*

VANESSA: Oh, thank you, that's just what I need—

ISMAEL: *Listen, este, you want someone to get you out of this? Maybe hit a few hot casinos in San Juan...?*

VANESSA: I'm seventeen.

ISMAEL: *My grandmother was seventeen when she gave birth to my father—*

(VANESSA *shoves* ISMAEL *and his chainsaw out to the porch.*)

ISMAEL: Good. I'll come by tonight. I'm taking you to La Quince. Wear something sexy! (*He exits.*)

(*With nothing else to do,* VANESSA *puts her headphones on and walks around the house smashing bugs.*)

Scene Two

(*Gorgeous sunset. Streetlights, porch lights, and the T V are on.*)

(*Coquis chirp. The windows and doors are closed, locked. The living room floor is clean.*)

(ADORACIÓN *lurks.*)

(BELEN, *on the sofa, watches T V.*)

(VANESSA *sits next to* BELEN. *She's changed her clothes and looks less foreign. She's on her cell-phone, leaving a message for her mother.*)

VANESSA: I helped the old lady make rice and beans. I washed her floor. I took a walk and saw nothing but dead baby cows, radar dishes, massive vegetation. Oh, but, I found a mango tree and I stuffed myself, hmm! Then I watched a tarantula TAKE AN HOUR to cross the street. At sundown, the old lady makes me come

inside, then she locks the doors and windows like it's
Rikers Island! I'm stuck watching Bonanza and Gomer
Pyle so I went in the bathroom and masturbated,
okay?? That's right, Ma, the word "masturbated" is on
your machine—twice! Day One and I have exhausted
my imagination on this place. It's a prison and I want
out. Call me, Flo, tell me you've made arrangements.
(She turns off the phone.)

(From a distance, in the dark, a cuatro plays—a sweet, old
jibaro melody.)

(A young man appears wearing a gold, tinfoil crown, a long
tattered purple robe, and a bad, fake beard.)

(He sings a folk ballad celebrating Three Kings Day.)

(Upon hearing the music, BELEN grabs the machete and
rushes out to the porch with it. She calls to VANESSA who
stares dully at the T V.)

BELEN: Ay, listen to that, child! They don't play music
like that in Paterson! (Sings and dances along.) Yes,
Cheo, you remember the sacred days.

(The singer finishes his song. He is KEVIN ALEJANDRO
BETANCES, twenty-six, A K A CHEO.)

(BELEN reaches into her bosom and takes out a dollar, which
she puts in the tin cup CHEO has strapped to his belt.)

CHEO: My angel, my inspiration, the First Lady of
Puerto Rico!

(BELEN kisses CHEO.)

BELEN: My son, why are you alone? I seem to
remember there were three Wise Men...

CHEO: Can you believe it? I went from house to house,
I couldn't find two people to be the other kings. They'd
rather be watching Bonanza.

BELEN: We live in the dark ages, my sweet son.

CHEO: Not for long. I promise you. *(Shows the dollar she gave him.)* This will help.

BELEN: Just be careful. I hear the F B I is everywhere. They put you in jail and experiment on your genitals.

(Drawn by the voices, bored with T V, VANESSA comes out to the porch, sees CHEO in his absurd costume, and laughs.)

CHEO: *(To BELEN)* I'm sorry, I didn't know you had company...

BELEN: My great-granddaughter from Paterson, God help me.

(CHEO takes off the fake beard and crown. His face is dark, angular, with intense, melancholy eyes.)

(VANESSA tries not to show that she notices how good-looking CHEO is.)

CHEO: *(Smiles, to VANESSA)* So? Didn't you enjoy the music? Where's your dollar for the cause?

BELEN: *(To VANESSA)* This is Cheo. He and his followers are doing important work for the island. I hear fewer coquis every night and Cheo's going to change that.

CHEO: *(To VANESSA)* Mass extinction. It's the sewage they pour in our lagoons, instead of the beaches, where the tourists go. Doña Belen won't listen, but I think it was pollution that caused her miscarriages.

BELEN: Atheist!

CHEO: Surely you want to help out, miss.

BELEN: Vanessa doesn't speak the language. A Puerto Rican without language is a ghost.

(When CHEO switches from English to Spanish and back, we hear NO CHANGE in accent.)

CHEO: *(To VANESSA)* Not a single word?

VANESSA: I've had a long day, Pancho. Long. Day.

CHEO: The name's Cheo, and what's wrong with you? Why don't you speak Spanish?

BELEN: *(Impatient)* Ay, tell her about the coqui! The tragedy!

CHEO: *(To* VANESSA*)* That chirping you hear, that's the coqui. Tree frog about the size of—

BELEN: *(Delighted)* Tell her about the *Elulutherodoodle-cacalo...*

CHEO: *(To* VANESSA*)* The coqui is the symbol of Puerto Rico. We have sixteen different species. The most common is the *Eleutherodactylus coqui*—

BELEN: *(Delighted)* A-hah! That one!

CHEO: But on this side of the island we have mostly *Eleutherodactylus antillencis*. They're all dying out, every species. In the last twenty years, we've lost the Golden Coqui, Eneida's Coqui, and Coqui Palmeado...gone forever.

VANESSA: *(Re his clothes)* What the hell's that?

CHEO: Don't you know? *(To* BELEN*)* I bet she's never even heard of Three Kings Day!

BELEN: *(To* CHEO*)* I bet she can tell you where to buy marijuana.

VANESSA: *(Excited, to* CHEO*)* Did she say marijuana?

CHEO: *(Trying to stay patient)* Do you even know what this island's going through right now? The election we're about to have?

VANESSA: I know I heard marijuana.

BELEN: She'd make a challenging wife, Cheo... *(Looking at* VANESSA*'s ass.)* ...but we'd have to work on that ass.

CHEO: *(Looking)* Yeah. Little bony.

BELEN: After a month of my cooking, *bendito*, that ass is going to be as round and ripe as a—

CHEO: ...mango, no, papaya, no, like a, like a...

VANESSA: Hey, if you're gonna talk about my ass, do it in English.

(CHEO *jumps on the porch and speaks as if before a crowd.*)

CHEO: "If Puerto Rico votes to become a state of the United States, we will be shitting on our past and performing an absurdest tragedy worthy of Jean Genet!" That's from the speech I gave in Arecibo last week.

VANESSA: Boring.

CHEO: Half this barrio thinks I'm crazy, the other half ignores me but the sad truth is, in five hundred years, we've been a free people for only a week and a day. And that has to change. *(To* BELEN*)* Right? Independence?

BELEN: Long live the free, democratic Republic of Puerto Rico!

CHEO: *(To* VANESSA*)* See? My people know! In their instincts!

BELEN: *(To* VANESSA*)* He's going to be president some day, you watch!

CHEO: *(Encouraged, to* VANESSA*)* Our cause is dedicated to the memory of Pedro Albizu Campos. Do you know what the U S did to that genius? Stuck him like a dog in a prison...roasted him alive with radiation injected directly into his body. You can read all about him on our website, usoutofpuertorico.com.

ISMAEL: *(Off) All that about Albizu Campos is bullshit—*

(ISMAEL *appears out of the darkness, dressed nicely.*)

BELEN: *(Dreading a fight between the men, to* CHEO*)* Play something sweet by Los Reyes de la Plena. Or Trio Boricua.

CHEO: *(To* ISMAEL*)* You just don't want to believe what your precious U S A is capable of—

ISMAEL: *That rumor was never proven, Kevin.*

VANESSA: *(To* CHEO*)* Kevin? I thought it was Cheo.

CHEO: *(To* VANESSA*)* Kevin Alejandro Betances. No relation to the great freedom-fighter...

ISMAEL: *But he calls himself Cheo because "Che" was already taken.*

CHEO: *(Angry, to* ISMAEL*)* Don't you have to bomb Vieques or something?

BELEN: No—you are *both* my angels—no fighting—

ISMAEL: *I came to see if Vanessa wants to go to La Quince. We could get some beers, listen to the Stones, shoot pool...*

CHEO: *(To* VANESSA, *laughing)* Lucky Vanessa. About to experience the joy of sex with Tio Taco...

BELEN: *(Alarmed)* You were like brothers, and it breaks my heart—

ISMAEL: *(Angry, to* CHEO*) Look, take your doomed, dead, nationalistic bullshit and get lost, Kevin. It's sad the way you hold on to this. It's over. Statehood's going to win. Time to forget these romantic ideas of a "nation" called Puerto Rico.*

CHEO: *(To* VANESSA*)* He can't stand it. The thought of Puerto Rico being free.

ISMAEL: *The U S gave him everything and he hates it. But ask him what the life expectancy was before the U S came in. Thirty-five years. Now it's seventy.*

CHEO: Seventy years of grinding poverty, disease, exploitation, political limbo...oh, sign me up.

ISMAEL: *(To* CHEO*) Come on, bro, do you really think, after all this time, the U S can just pull out of Puerto Rico?*

CHEO: Why not?

ISMAEL: *We need statehood to save us from ourselves. Rene Marques was right about us, we're docile, politically apathetic...* (Anticipating CHEO's response) *After five hundred years of—?*

CHEO: (Overlapping) After five hundred years of colonial rule? What the hell do you—?

ISMAEL: *I give up, you win.* (To VANESSA) *Let's go.*

CHEO: No, no, no—you gotta tell me something, Izzy—I want to know how the U S can tolerate a state full of people who don't want to be a state.

ISMAEL: *I don't know, bro, ask Alaska, ask Hawaii.*

CHEO: Ask Quebec.

ISMAEL: *Will you shut up and let me take Vanessa to La Quince!?*

CHEO: (Imitating ISMAEL) Here, Uncle Sam, here are my balls. I don't know how to use them. Maybe you could teach me, sir. (Playful, to VANESSA) C'mon, give me a point for that...

(VANESSA *laughs.*)

ISMAEL: (Angry, to CHEO) *Here's what it comes down to. What's going to happen the day after independence? Well, first, everyone on the island will lose their U.S. citizenship. Then anyone with half an education will book a flight to Ohio. Then we're going to realize that we don't have free access to the U S markets anymore. Then our pretty new currency with the pretty little face of Pedro Albizu Campos will collapse.*

CHEO: (Anticipating his argument) And then we're going to starve to death.

ISMAEL: (Overlapping) *And then we're going to starve to death—that's right.*

CHEO: The old "starve to death." *Compai,* it's a tropical island. Shit grows here.

ISMAEL: *You know there's not enough land or skill in Puerto Rico—*

CHEO: The Tainos did it. With no technology. And we could do it too if every decent acre hadn't been stolen by the Empire in the name of King Sugar.

ISMAEL: *(Laughs) "Empire?" "King Sugar?" Wow. Just wow.*

CHEO: And you know for a fact the independence parties are asking for a long transition, with enough foreign aid—

ISMAEL: *Why the fuck should the U S give us a penny after we reject the gift of statehood?*

CHEO: Payback for all the wealth their corporations took?

ISMAEL: *You believe in fairy tales, bro. I believe in eight new members of the House of Representatives and two Senators: that's the real prize. Right now, Cheo, any pig-faced redneck Senator from Mississippi can decide what life in Puerto Rico should be like. I'd love to see a Puerto Rican Senator changing life in Mississippi.*

VANESSA: *(To* ISMAEL*)* Slam dunk!

CHEO: *(Dismissive)* All he's getting is a ton of new federal and state taxes and a complete loss of dignity.

ISMAEL: *So full of shit. We'd have much more dignity as a state. We earned this. We paid a blood tax in all the U S wars. My grandfather paid the ultimate price in France. Two uncles in Vietnam. Statehood is a gift paid for by our dead. Statehood is a moral imperative.*

CHEO: Statehood is the murder of a nation.

ISMAEL: *Me cago on that argument! You have a utopia in your head: happy jibaros in their shacks of straw, wearing pavas, on their mules, free to dance their coplas and decimas, to pray to Las Siete Potencias, and make babies. This island*

nearly starved in the thirties and forties. Look at the pictures.
Malaria, hookworm, malnutrition. It's in the eyes. In those
doomed jibaro eyes you love to romanticize.

CHEO: *(To* VANESSA*)* You know why he believes in
statehood?

ISMAEL: *Now? We're happy, got our malls, Toyotas, easy*
Internet access. It's called progress, you Commie, Fidel-
loving fuck!

CHEO: *(To* VANESSA*)* He works in real estate. He thinks
the property values will skyrocket if we go statehood.
But he loves to forget that most North Americans don't
want us in their precious country!

BELEN: My father was killed the day of the gringo
invasion!

(CHEO *and* ISMAEL *go silent as they look at* BELEN, *who*
tries not to cry.)

BELEN: My mother watched the soldiers walk through
Arecibo, laughing, like it was a joke, a picnic. We put
up almost no resistance—except for Papi. He fired
his old pistol, wounded himself in the foot, and they
turned their rifles on him and decorated his valor with
their bullets.

(CHEO *and* ISMAEL *go to comfort* BELEN.)

ISMAEL: *(To* CHEO*) You made her cry.*

CHEO: *(To* ISMAEL*)* You made her cry.

VANESSA: *(To* BELEN*)* You okay?

(VANESSA *strokes* BELEN's *hair until* BELEN *smiles.)*

BELEN: *(To* VANESSA*)* Okay.

(CHEO *and* ISMAEL *go silent, their anger and indignation*
temporarily spent as they hold BELEN.)

(VANESSA *looks at the two passionate young men fighting for her attention. Maybe being in Puerto Rico won't be so bad...*)

VANESSA: Okay. *(To* ISMAEL*)* ...I hope you shoot pool as good as you talk, bro.

ISMAEL: *I'm your man!*

(VANESSA *and* ISMAEL *disappear in the darkness.*)

(CHEO, *comforting* BELEN, *watches* VANESSA *and* ISMAEL *disappear, then walks* BELEN *into the house.*)

Scene Three

(*Later. The sofa in the living room has been made up for* VANESSA *to sleep on. The T V is on.*)

(CHEO *is asleep in the rocking chair, on the porch.*)

(ADORACIÓN *has been in bed with* BELEN *for hours, kissing her on the cheek, gently stroking her long hair.*)

(BELEN *stares at the ceiling, rigid with anger and insomnia.*)

ADORACIÓN: ...No, Don Toli wasn't the strongest man in Las Arenas. But you never measure a man's true strength by the amount of suffering he can take or the amount of cane he can cut in a day or how many shots of rum it takes to make him smile after a day of hard labor. When I took water to the men in the fields, or filled my *fiambrera* with hot *asopao*, I treated each man like he was a king. I knew work was scarce and soon the *tiempo muerto* would come and the *guajana* would cover the fields and there would be no work for nine months and much suffering. Yes, women whispered that I was a whore because I went to those fields to refresh the men with water and soup, even though I had no husband, or *novio*, and a girl my age was never allowed alone in those fields with all those men. But I didn't care about the rumors and dirty words! Those

men were heroes in my eyes, each one, not mules like
the foremen thought. Each man was a soldier fighting
against the starvation that always seemed only a day
or two away. It shocked me that every woman in Las
Arenas wasn't out there with me. The nerve of those
bitches calling me whore! *(Beat)* The first time I gave
Don Toli his water, I knew. How a man can work
under the hot sun, bent like an animal and still have
the willpower for sexy thoughts is beyond me. He took
my water. And, later, he took the rest of me without
lifting a finger. Sometimes you come face to face with
your definition of manhood. Not your mother's, not
your religion's, not your barrio's. Yours. And I did.

(BELEN slaps ADORACIÓN across the face.)

(ADORACIÓN feels no pain and doesn't react.)

*(BELEN slaps her again and again: and again there's no
reaction.)*

*(In frustration, BELEN gets out of bed, goes to the sofa,
collapses.)*

(VANESSA and ISMAEL approach the porch.)

ISMAEL: *(Laughs, to VANESSA)* Your guard dog's waiting.
Don't you feel safer?

(CHEO wakes up, regards them darkly.)

CHEO: Doña couldn't sleep because of the ghost. I told
her I'd stick around.

ISMAEL: *(Knowing why he's really there)* Uh-huh. Don't
you have to bomb the people who bomb Vieques?

CHEO: Ours is a nonviolent movement, Izzy, like...

ISMAEL: *...like Gandhi and Cesar Chavez and blah blah blah.
(To VANESSA) Call me if you need anything. I work Monday
to Thursday, then I'm free. I'm the house with the American
flag on the second floor. The one with fifty-one stars. I*

*could take you to old San Juan, Luquillo Beach, Ponce, El
Yunque—*

CHEO: The next couple of weeks could be a bad time to
travel.

ISMAEL: *(To* CHEO) *Was I directing this statement to you?
(To Vanessa) You tell me, I'll take you, okay? I got friends
that will keep us safe. And tell him to keep his hands to
himself. Bye.*

VANESSA: You should talk.

(ISMAEL *exits.)*

(CHEO *and* VANESSA *look at each other, awkward.)*

(VANESSA *looks at the night sky, listens to the coquis.)*

CHEO: While you're in Puerto Rico, you should take a
real good look around. Before it's too late. And don't
do it with Izzy—he only knows what the tourists
know. Promise me you'll do that?

VANESSA: Why's it so important to you?

CHEO: Because all this is gonna be gone some day.
Little neighborhoods like Las Arenas, their little
plots of land, full of chickens and pigs, this semi-
independent way of life...it's all disappearing, like the
coqui...getting buried...as the highways get closer. Even
the stories told by old women like Doña Belen, the
stories that hold these barrios together and connect the
past with the present...all that's dying.

VANESSA: *(Looking around)* Looks to me like it ain't
changed since the Jurassic Period.

(CHEO *looks at her, wondering how much he can confide.)*

CHEO: There was a place I used to swim in, when I
was a kid. On the beach, outside Arecibo, beautiful
little bay called La Posa. It was my spot. Diving off the
rocks. Time would stop for us. Black kids, white kids,
we were one color: the color of fish. And the ocean was

our home. The sun was our clock. Nobody was hungry in that water. Nobody was ignorant. I used to think... it must've been like this for the Tainos: perfect, pure, endless. One day I walked there...there's a fence. La Posa was bought by a U S hotel chain and the thing that was mine—and all us kids—was out of reach. For the fucking rich tourists.

(VANESSA *studies* CHEO's *face a long moment.*)

CHEO: I hated that fence. Made my hands and feet bloody trying to do Kung-Fu on it. Begged Doña Belen to hit it with a curse. But La Posa died. When I stopped breaking my hands, I went home to think and I realized the only way out of this was nonviolent political action. That's all I've thought about. Now I'm a month away from finding out if I wasted my life.

VANESSA: Izzy was saying, every time there's an election your side only gets like three percent.

CHEO: I think I know my people, Vanessa. And we're so damn *restless*, so ready for a new concept of home, we're on the verge of exploding! Something's going to be born next month. The question is what.

(VANESSA *doesn't answer right away. She studies him again.*)

VANESSA: You know, you don't seem that Puerto Rican to me.

(CHEO *thinks about this, wondering how honest to be with her.*)

CHEO: *(Reluctant)* I went to a prep school in New Hampshire...then I went to Columbia. But I couldn't stay up there. After graduation I hooked up with my old friends. Night after night talking about change, *real* change, not a *theory* of change, and *now*, not waiting for the next generation to save our ass, like our parents waited. I got a bicycle and rode from one end of the island to the other. Took me a year.

(*Beat*)

VANESSA: You ever take a night off from the Crusade? 'Cause I think what we gotta do is climb that fence, say fuck you to the tourists, and swim naked in La Posa tomorrow night. Tell me that ain't revolutionary.

CHEO: (*Surprised, pleased*) That sounds cool, but I have to be at a rally in Ponce tomorrow night—

VANESSA: Day after?

CHEO: I'd like to but I need to spend every minute this month organizing to get out the vote.

VANESSA: So there's no way to get together and break a few rules around here?

CHEO: Why don't you work with me? On the campaign. I lead a small non-violent cell, twelve of us share a house in Arecibo, we're the *Grito de Lares* Movement. Twelve people trying to do the work of a hundred. North-central Puerto Rico is my precinct—

VANESSA: I don't even speak *Español*!

CHEO: It doesn't have to be a lot. Stuff envelopes, hand out flyers in the plaza—

VANESSA: (*Teasing*) No, stop, that sounds too hot.

CHEO: Come on, you're a Puerto Rican woman, this is your country calling!

VANESSA: My country is Jersey!

CHEO: *Pero todavia lleva la mancha de platano!*

VANESSA: Like I even know what that means, Cheo!

CHEO: You're scared. I'm scared too. You don't know how many death threats we get every week.

VANESSA: Your skills as a salesman, whoa...

CHEO: Come on, you'd be on a tropical island, having an adventure.

VANESSA: *(Beat)* It's just...how do you know you're right? What if Izzy's right and you get freedom and you starve to death? Isn't that possible?

(CHEO *takes a breath. This isn't going to work. Or has she hit a subconscious fear of his?)*

(*He leans over and kisses* VANESSA *softly on the cheek, surprising her.)*

CHEO: It's good Doña Belen has family with her, she's lonely. But I have a shit-load of work to do and no time. I'm sorry you won't be with me. I just hope you find yourself connected to this place, because it's in you. It might even be the best part of you.

VANESSA: You're pissed at me.

CHEO: I'm sorry. This isn't a game. Or a T V show. Or a costume drama we natives are putting on for the tourists. *(Beat)* I'll see you again when we're free. *(He exits.)*

(VANESSA *watches* CHEO *leave. Disappointed,* VANESSA *goes into the house, sees* BELEN *asleep on the sofa. Watches her. Adjusts her blanket)*

(*In her sleep,* BELEN *"talks" to Don Toli.)*

BELEN: *(In her sleep)* I don't want to get pregnant any more, Toli. *(As Toli)* What are you talking about, Belen, shut up. *(As herself)* It's not that I don't want to make love! *(As Toli)* It's a sin to talk to your husband about making love! Stop it! *(As herself)* But when I'm pregnant...I'm not me anymore...I'm God's servant... delivering another soul to the world. I can't eat and everything makes me vomit and it feels like a war in my womb...why does God put the seed in my belly and make my body fight it? What acid, what poison, do I shower on the fetus, suffocating her and stopping her heart? Why did God give me seven? Why did God erase them? Ay, no more, Toli, no. Let's silence our passion and be like brother and sister from now on. I'll cook and honor and care for you. I'll doctor your wounds and sing away your nightmares. I'll be your wall and your sanctuary: God will never find fault with our love, Toli. He'll know its purity is as clean as any marriage, like Mary and Joseph, even if we never touch each other again. *(As Toli)* You talk like a witch. I'm a man, Belen, and I must have what a man must have. I won't have the men of Las Arenas think less of me. This house will have a child. Bless me, Belen. *(As herself)* May God bless you, Toli. *(As Toli)* Again. *(As herself)* May God in his Infinite Compassion embrace you, Toli, and bless your home with children, children, children.

(VANESSA *goes to the bedroom and sits on the bed.*)

(ADORACIÓN *sits with her.*)

(VANESSA *lies on the bed.*)

(ADORACIÓN *lies with her.*)

(VANESSA *can sense her. She fights her impulse to flee in terror.*)

VANESSA: Adoración?

ADORACIÓN: Welcome to Las Arenas, angel.

(VANESSA *sits up, gasps.*)

(*Black out.*)

END OF ACT ONE

ACT TWO

Scene One

(A month later)

(The house is clean and decorated with Puerto Rican flags. Banners proclaim: "Vota por Independencia!", "Nacionalismo Si! Annexacion No!" etc.)

(In the dark, CHEO's voice:)

CHEO: *(Off. Singing)*
Despierta, borinqueño,
que han dado la señal!
Despierta de ese sueño
que es hora de luchar!

(The quiet barrio has changed. In the distance we hear firecrackers, campaign music from rival camps, political speeches delivered on loudspeakers on passing cars, shouts, cheers, helicopters, fighter jets, the rumble of heavy vehicles.)

(The sounds rise in volume, hit a peak, then die down.)

(BELEN lies in her bed, very ill.)

(ADORACIÓN lurks.)

(VANESSA sits at BELEN's side, spoon-feeding BELEN asopao. VANESSA hums the song CHEO sang when they met and eats slices of mango with great relish.)

(VANESSA is subtly changed. Her clothes and hair resemble ADORACIÓN. She has an easier, sexier manner. She's put on a few pounds and wears no make-up.)

BELEN: *(Very ill, labored)* There was a time I was considered the most beautiful girl in the world. I could perform miracles with my beauty. Cure diseases, inspire poets. I have those poems here somewhere, but I think I lost them, shit! Scientists from around the world came to Las Arenas to study me, the reincarnation of Helen of Troy, may God protect that heathen bitch.

VANESSA: *(Halting, heavily-accented) My little-grandma... many, many beauty...*

BELEN: *(To* VANESSA*)* And arrogant! No man alive could get near me. From the time I was twelve, I shunned them all, put them in their place, old men, sexy men, powerful men...

VANESSA: *Soup good? Hungry more good?*

BELEN: Only one man was unmoved by my magic. He was quiet and modest, my reputation and charm meant nothing. And I fell for that sneaky motherfucker so fast, it wasn't even funny.

*(*VANESSA *can see there's no way she can make* BELEN *eat.)*

VANESSA: *Water?*

BELEN: Rum.

VANESSA: *Water.*

*(*VANESSA *goes off to get* BELEN *water.)*

*(*ADORACIÓN *approaches* BELEN*.)*

ADORACIÓN: Why do you hold on to this miserable life? Look at you. You're a ghoul. You were never that beautiful to begin with! I was. Even your parents said so! And I'm still beautiful. My skin doesn't drag on the ground. My hair is full of wind and sunshine. Put your hand between my legs. I didn't dry up!

BELEN: *(Weak, re* VANESSA*)* Do you see how she takes care of me...?

ADORACIÓN: *(Ignoring that)* People say the dead walk the earth because we have unfinished business. But sometimes it's the *living* who keep us here with their unfinished work. Fights they should have had. Revelations that came too late. Lovers they can't let go. What do you want to learn from me, you old whore, that you don't already know? Why do you keep me here? Huh? You won't die, you won't let me go, you won't let me talk to Vanessa...

BELEN: *(Weak)* When I die, Vanessa will say such beautiful things at my funeral...

ADORACIÓN: *(Fierce)* After I died, Don Toli would leave your bed at night and walk to my grave, crying the whole way!

BELEN: *(Violent)* Liar! He danced on your grave!

ADORACIÓN: *(Grabbing BELEN roughly)* I gave you this fever. The bloody diarrhea. I'm in your guts like a worm. Slowly melting each of your bones. But it's not fast enough. Maybe this will do it...

(ADORACIÓN *kisses* BELEN *full on the mouth and gropes her.)*

(BELEN *nearly suffocates in the violent kiss. She struggles and pushes* ADORACIÓN *away.)*

(BELEN *stumbles to the off-stage bathroom and vomits.)*

(*Alarmed by the noise,* VANESSA *comes back on, holding a glass of water. She can hear* BELEN *in the bathroom, throwing up.)*

(CHEO *enters and approaches the porch. Exhausted, unshaven, he's been working nonstop all month and hasn't slept in three days.)*

(VANESSA's *back is to him as she listens, concerned, outside* BELEN's *bathroom.)*

CHEO: Vanessa?

(VANESSA *turns around to see him, pleased, relieved, as he is. Time has only intensified the attraction.*)

VANESSA: I'm good, thanks for asking. Yes its been a lonely month, thanks for calling, thanks for stopping by—

CHEO: Be nice. I haven't slept in three days...

VANESSA: You look it. So you finished all the great work?

CHEO: All I know is it's the last day. When the polls close at nine, that's it. It's literally history.

VANESSA: Came by to say hi to the girl in the *haunted house*? Hearing voices at night? And crying!

CHEO: I came to take Doña Belen to vote. And to say hi to Vanessa...who looks like she's quite at home, ghosts and all.

VANESSA: Learned how to make *sofrito*, oh, that *mofongo*, man, that *pernil*, I could O D on that shit.

CHEO: Even pronounced it right.

VANESSA: So you sticking around this time or do you gotta liberate the Virgin Islands too?

CHEO: Tonight I'm going to the safe house in Arecibo to watch the returns on T V. Would you like to go to Arecibo with me—?

VANESSA: Actually, yeah I would, but great-grandma's sick, I gotta stay—

CHEO: What's wrong?

VANESSA: Fever, the shits, but she says not to worry.

CHEO: You understand her?

VANESSA: Picked up a couple of words. Another month and I'd be speaking at the university level.

CHEO: Impress me.

VANESSA: *(Haltingly) The sky is blue. The beans are cold.*

CHEO: Complete sentences...

VANESSA: *The little pink ducks are homosexual.*

(CHEO *laughs.*)

VANESSA: *(Looking him over)* Ay, this tropical heat! On every inch there's something alive, something eating, or fighting, or fucking. Like a feast and a funeral all the time. Makes me have strange yearnings. *(Sexy smile)* God gives us a body to use. A voice to scream it. Legs to encircle. Hips to bear the weight.

CHEO: That's an interesting thing to say...

(A fighter jet streaks across the sky over them.)

VANESSA: Wild, huh? Fighter jets. Those riots in Ponce, man, I couldn't believe those.

CHEO: You heard about that?

VANESSA: I was there! Just after it happened. Went to San Juan...oh, met these students who said, like, the U S Navy's gonna surround the island if independence wins.

CHEO: My friends in the New Nationalist Party heard the U S Congress is going to annul the vote if it's not statehood.

VANESSA: And there's some army...in the rain forest...?

CHEO: A guerilla army in El Yunque, planning an assault on San Juan if we become the fifty-first state. They say they've got caves filled with machetes. Gonna turn El Yunque into the next Sierra Maestra.

(A moment as VANESSA looks at CHEO.)

VANESSA: A couple of days ago, I caught a car to Arecibo...finally found La Posa. I saw the fence. Tried to picture this skinny little angry boy doing Kung-Fu, beating his hands all bloody.

CHEO: And his feet.

VANESSA: *(Beat)* I was kinda hoping I'd run into you out there....

CHEO: When things settle down, you and I are going to steal some time, and I'm going to take you to the places on the island the tourists never see. You're not going to believe your eyes.

(VANESSA *walks away from* CHEO.)

VANESSA: But I'm going home next week. I'm leaving Puerto Rico.

CHEO: Just when you're starting to feel at home—?

VANESSA: Cheo, my Papi's in trouble again. He's got some problems with drugs and he's been in and out of jail—

CHEO: But the next few months, after there's independence...

(VANESSA *wipes her eyes.*)

VANESSA: My father is still a child. He got high and punched me in the mouth on my birthday because I was wearing *shorts* and all I could do was laugh at him—all the blood between my teeth tasted like salt sea-water—the same blood I spit in his face. It's why my mother sent me out here...to protect me from all that. But she can't handle things alone and she needs me to come back.

CHEO: *(He goes to her, holds her tightly, then kisses her, mouths lingering gently together.)* This month I shook a thousand hands, gave out flags, drank Don Q with old timers with stories of Don Pedro...but sometimes all I wanted was to hear you mangle the Spanish language, and to try your burnt tostones.

VANESSA: *(Holding him)* Bet you wanted to try my tostones...

(VANESSA *kisses* CHEO, *longer, more.*)

(BELEN *shuffles into the living room.*)

BELEN: Sweet angels...when's the wedding?

(VANESSA *and* CHEO *pull apart.*)

CHEO: How do you feel?

BELEN: Who cares? I'm one person. A speck of sand on God's beach. A teardrop in His eyes—

CHEO: *(Going to her)* I care about you—

BELEN: No, no, bigger things are happening. Are we going to kick those gringos out or what?

CHEO: We're going to try.

(VANESSA *grabs* BELEN's *sweater and Bible*)

BELEN: All our brothers and sisters...migrating north to get rich, leaving us to starve and wait. Marriages, deaths, births, baptisms...all happened in Philadelphia, and Newark and Lower East Side. Not on the land that conceived them. Why couldn't they put their sweat and sacrifice into *this* land? Why did they ruin their minds in a place that compared them to cockroaches? So bright, young, hopeful...kidnapped by advertising, imprisoned by snow, buried alive in bricks and subways.

CHEO: *(To BELEN)* Are you ready to do this?

BELEN: I may be dying but that won't stop me from fighting for my country against General Electric, Westinghouse, and the Presbyterian Church! Señor, save us from the Dark Ages and protect us from their Ricky Martins!

CHEO: Let's go, angel. Let's make history.

(BELEN *clasps her hands.*)

BELEN: Precious God, give us strength...be our liberator tonight...and you will see the most grateful nation the world has ever known. Amen.

(CHEO, VANESSA, *and* BELEN *leave*.)

(*Firecrackers, horns honking, shouts.*)

Scene Two

(*That night*)

(VANESSA *is riveted to the T V. The light and noise of the T V fill the room.*)

(*Sicker than ever,* BELEN *sits on the sofa next to* VANESSA. BELEN'*s stomach hurts.*)

BELEN: Ay, that damn bitch did it...she put worms in my insides...

VANESSA: (*Torn between the T V and* BELEN) Do you want something to eat? Food, eat?

BELEN: Vanessa, you've been so good to me...and I knew you'd be good to me because you're my Celia's granddaughter. We could be separated by mountains and generations yet the blood we have is strong! (*She starts to cry.*)

VANESSA: Hey, hey, no.

BELEN: (*To* VANESSA, *weak, afraid*) Please, Vanessa, don't let me die. Don't let Adoración take my life, Vanessa, please don't let her!

VANESSA: (*To* BELEN) If you could just slow down a little—

BELEN: (*To* VANESSA) None of my organs work. My eyes see shadows and nothing else. I've started to shit myself.

VANESSA: Slower, slower...

BELEN: But I don't want to let this go. I don't want to
face God. I don't want him to judge my sins!

VANESSA: *Doctor? Please? Doctor?*

BELEN: Fuck doctors! They waste your time and steal
your hope and help themselves to everything in the
bank!

VANESSA: No doctors, check.

BELEN: Do you know how many Hail Marys I've said
in my life? How many rosary beads I've worn down
to nothing? All for what? God's never going to see the
soul of the woman who did all those things.

(The sound of gunshots outside the house.)

BELEN: What the hell's that?

*(Before she can answer, a sound on the T V gets VANESSA's
and BELEN's attention.)*

VANESSA: *(Watching T V)* Oh shit, here it comes. Look!
The news!

BELEN: *(Trying to focus on the T V)* All my life, elections
were shown in Spanish! Why does this one have to be
in English?

VANESSA: *(Responding to the T V)* Little-grandma, you see
what happened? *The street—people sing—dance.* Wild!
Tanks...battleships.

BELEN: Did we win? Is Cheo president?

(BELEN and VANESSA watch the T V in silence, then...)

VANESSA: *(Indicating the T V)* Oh my God. Oh fuck! No!

BELEN: *(Looking at the T V)* Who is that ugly man?

VANESSA: That's the President of the United States.

BELEN: What the hell's he doing?

VANESSA: Celebrating 'cause his country just got a little bigger. *(Beat)* Fifty-two percent of the people of Puerto Rico went for statehood. Independence...got...three.

BELEN: *(Looking at the T V)* We lost?

VANESSA: Killed.

BELEN: *(Sinking in)* What? We *lost*?

VANESSA: The polls are closed. Yes. It's official. Look. There's the new American flag. With fifty-one stars.

(BELEN *clasps her hands.*)

BELEN: Ay! Endure, endure, little island.

(VANESSA *turns off the T V and turns on her cellphone. She calls* CHEO.)

BELEN: *(In prayer)* Take your peace where you can find it. Remember yourself. Go inside yourself. Under the soil. In the old songs and poems. We are not slaves, dear God. We are not slaves. Ay, poor Cheo!

VANESSA: You know where he is? *Where? Cheo?*

BELEN: That poor boy, poor son of Puerto Rico.

VANESSA: I've been trying his cell—

BELEN: *(Points to cupboard)* Get me something to drink. *(Mimes)* Drink.

VANESSA: *Sleeping. Please sleeping, you.*

BELEN: *(Fierce)* I said DRINK and I mean NOW and I mean RUM!

VANESSA: *(Almost laughs)* At your service, ma'am.

(VANESSA *gets* BELEN *a rum and two shot glasses. They take shots.*)

BELEN: *(Stronger)* I will not, I will not, I will not be a North American.

(*Gunshots. Shouts. Loud cars*)

VANESSA: They're going crazy.

(BELEN *crosses to the door.*)

BELEN: Ill-mannered, poorly-raised, snot-nosed—

VANESSA: *Little-grandma,* what're you—?

(BELEN *opens the door and limps out to the porch.*)

(VANESSA *follows.*)

BELEN: *(Shouting to offstage people)* What's wrong with all of you? Don't you know what you've given away? Tonight you should be home! With your children! Thinking about the future! What kind of Puerto Rico have we become? What does it mean to be the fifty-first state of the United States?

(*Gunshots subside. Cars drive away.*)

(*A total silence we haven't heard before.*)

VANESSA: Something weird out here.

BELEN: *(Crossing herself)* The coquis have stopped singing...

(BELEN *and* VANESSA *listen to the strange silence and involuntarily draw closer together.*)

Scene Three

(*Later, just before sunrise.* BELEN *lies on the sofa, the bottle of rum in her hand.*)

(VANESSA *sits on the porch, asleep on the rocking chair.*)

(CHEO *appears. He's exhausted, a little drunk, animated by anger and self-pity. He holds a half-empty bottle of rum.*)

CHEO: Congratulations, America! You're on a roll!

(VANESSA *awakens, looks at* CHEO.)

VANESSA: Thank God you're alive...

(VANESSA *goes to* CHEO, *embraces him.*)

(CHEO *pulls away, looks at* VANESSA.)

CHEO: Why do you even want to be with me? Why should anyone give a fuck what I have to say? I wasn't educated here. Never had a job here. Look at my clothes. I'm a walking colony! "My people." What a fucking joke. You know how many times I said "my people" in my life? I never got the dirt of Puerto Rico on my shoes. The air of this island swept through me, I never breathed it in. I swear on my mother's eyes, I'm right at the point where a bullet to the head looks pretty good—

VANESSA: Stop talking like that, c'mon.

CHEO: All of us in the house, you should've seen us, together like it's been for years, this family created around an *idea*, a *principle*, people who left marriages, sacrificed families, the hearts we broke. Last night we were broken. You could hear each spine snap. Couldn't even look at each other. Being Puerto Ricans we cried a lot. Some of us good atheists even said it was God's will.

VANESSA: Come to bed, you need the sleep...

CHEO: No! They have another star on their flag! Fifty used to be their magic number. So round. So clean. So North American. But now it's *past* fifty—the magic barrier is broken. How many little stars will they take after this? When will they stop? Until they have all the light? Until they own the sky?

(VANESSA *takes* CHEO's *bottle of rum.*)

VANESSA: All I'm saying, when the noise dies down, a little time passes, maybe it's gonna be clear this was the best thing that could have happened...

CHEO: *(Not listening)* We had a chance for something real...something that could free all the energy we've had locked up for five hundred years. To never again ask permission of the super-state to wipe our own ass. I swear, if there was a war tomorrow—and who knows, that's all I'm saying...I say: *take my body*. Take the whole thing, the legs, the balls: it's yours: I give it up to the cause now.

VANESSA: No cause is worth your balls!

CHEO: *Grito's* been my home all these years. But the New Nationalist Party wants me in their leadership. Some of them came to the house tonight...

VANESSA: Who are they?

ISMAEL: *(Off) The New Nationalists advocate violent military resistance to the United States.*

VANESSA: *(Quietly, to* CHEO*)* So you're telling me what?

ISMAEL: *(Off) What he's telling you is illegal.*

(ISMAEL *enters, a little drunk, wearing pro-statehood buttons and little American flags.)*

CHEO: Izzy, you picked the wrong goddamn time—

ISMAEL: *It's a great time. A great night to party! A great night for the United States and the cause of freedom and blah blah blah!*

VANESSA: For real, Ismael, you gotta—

ISMAEL: *(To* CHEO*) Bendito. Reality a little too hard to deal with, Cheo? The time to dream childish dreams is over, friend. Se 'cabo!*

CHEO: This vote does not represent the will of the Puerto Rican—

ISMAEL: *Not maybe your Puerto Ricans, but the sane Puerto Ricans—*

CHEO: Confusing ballots, polling mistakes, uncounted votes, people being turned away...

ISMAEL: *The U N Committee on De-Colonization supervised—*

CHEO: Like they're not in bed with the U S—

ISMAEL: *It's really hard when history passes you by, yet you cling to that rusty idea that once made sense to you, once kept you breathing...*

(CHEO *lunges at* ISMAEL. ISMAEL *is swift, strong and a full-out fight erupts.*)

(BELEN *comes out with a heavy sauce pan and beats both men with it until they stop fighting.*)

BELEN: This is what they want! This is what they want! We can just kill ourselves to make them happy!

(*There's blood on* CHEO's *face and* ISMAEL's *hands.* CHEO *lies on the ground motionless.*)

ISMAEL: (*To* VANESSA) *He's got nothing and he's going nowhere. He doesn't know how people laugh at him. Do you know what my future's going to be like? The doors that will open? Yeah, some people think I'm a joke. Ismael, the money man. Tio Taco. Mister Coconut: brown on the outside, white on the inside. I know you think so too. But I'm a serious man, Vanessa: and I want you with me in this incredible time.*

(*He leaves.*)

(BELEN *and* VANESSA *walk* CHEO *into the house.*)

(*They lay* CHEO *down on the sofa.*)

(VANESSA *lies next to* CHEO. *They hold each other.*)

(*Lying together on the sofa,* CHEO *and* VANESSA *kiss each other passionately.*)

(BELEN *leaves the living room and goes out to the porch.*)

(CHEO *and* VANESSA *begin to make love as the lights go to black.*)

Scene Four

(*Lights come up. A few days later*)

(BELEN *lies in bed, sleeping.*)

(ADORACIÓN *is at* BELEN's *side.*)

(CHEO *and* VANESSA *in the living room, getting dressed.*)

VANESSA: You're outta your mind, mister. I said no and no is no.

CHEO: You can't—*cielo*—you can't say no—

VANESSA: Think I can, think I did.

CHEO: It's just a meeting.

VANESSA: Oh really. Then why're people talking about bringing weapons?

CHEO: The police have weapons.

VANESSA: The police have weapons because people are rioting.

CHEO: Half the riots are police riots. They do the damage, shoot at people, we're the ones taking the bad press.

VANESSA: There's a curfew—

CHEO: Uh-huh, a curfew. Martial law. Summary arrests. Detention without trial. Political executions on the street in the name of law and order. A great first week as the fifty-first state!

VANESSA: Well, I don't support this. Those people who keep calling, I don't trust them.

CHEO: But everyone from *Grito* and *Sangre Libre* will be there. The Nationalists are electing officers. I've been nominated. What am I going to tell them? I can't be part of history because I'm in bed with my fucking girlfriend?

VANESSA: I know, in some universal female part of my gut, this is wrong for you. The militant way is not the way of the man I've been in bed with for a week. Who makes love better than anyone else. Am I right?

CHEO: Well, right.

VANESSA: Except this is not a culture that listens to its women, is my acute observation. Maybe you should put that in your constitution, huh?

CHEO: I'll make a note of it.

VANESSA: What you should do is say no to these people and start your own group—

CHEO: *(Getting frustrated)* Look, the Nationalists want all the independence parties to merge...then...go into hiding in El Yunque...and be part of the guerilla army.

VANESSA: And you're good with this?

CHEO: I've been thinking about it, yeah.

VANESSA: Why are you thinking of giving up on the nonviolence that was so important to you?

CHEO: Because we tried it and, oh my God, it didn't seem to work too good!

VANESSA: So they throw a free election at you and you throw back a bomb?

CHEO: How could that election be free? With their fucking warships parked outside San Juan, their guns aimed at us as we vote? When people think about that, and all the other shit the *yanquis* pulled, they're going to be mad enough to fight.

VANESSA: And that's you, huh? Mad enough to fight?

CHEO: This land's never spilled blood in a war for its own liberation. That might have to change. And very soon. *(Beat)* I'm going.

VANESSA: Then take me with you.

CHEO: No. Not even an option—

VANESSA: Because you know it's dangerous—

CHEO: I'm sorry. *(Beat)* I'll call as soon as it's over. *(Beat)* Take care of Doña Belen.

(CHEO *goes to kiss* VANESSA, *she pushes him away.)*

VANESSA: Fucking be careful.

(CHEO *leaves the house.)*

(VANESSA *watches* CHEO *disappear.)*

(BELEN *awakens, talks to herself.)*

BELEN: *(As herself)* The doctor said eat, Toli.

(VANESSA *enters* BELEN's *bedroom.)*

(ADORACIÓN *watches* VANESSA.)

(BELEN *speaks as Toli.)*

BELEN: For the sake of God and the goddamn nails in the feet of Christ, I don't want to eat. The cancer owns my stomach!

VANESSA: *Little-grandma?*

BELEN: *(As herself)* Eat, Toli. *(As Toli)* You're a deep, horrible woman, Belen, letting me die like this. To pretend to everyone you care about me. You always have my dinner ready. My clothes are always clean. You only want to get back at me for loving Adoración.

VANESSA: *Cheo. And me. Fighting.*

BELEN: *(As herself)* Eat, Toli. *(As Toli)* God alive! I'm the man you shared life with for fifty-four years! What could I do? You wouldn't touch me anymore—after all the miscarriages—you sinned first by denying me—you drove me to that girl, you did—you. Belen, precious, just say you forgive me one time and it's over. So I can die in peace. *(As herself)* Eat, Toli. *(As Toli)* It was decades ago, you cow! What are you holding on to? I'll be dead in a few days. It takes nothing away from you and I gain my soul. *(Long beat, as Toli)* You ugly, arrogant cunt! I shit on your eyes, Belen! I shit in your mouth! *(As herself)* Eat, Toli.

(VANESSA *gets into bed with* BELEN, *holds her.*)

(ADORACIÓN *whispers in* VANESSA's *ear.*)

ADORACIÓN: She never forgave Don Toli, Vanessa. She let him die in the worst way to die, so alone...

(VANESSA *sees* ADORACIÓN *and freezes.*)

(VANESSA *gets out of bed, pulling* BELEN *along with her.*)

Scene Five

(Next night. VANESSA *is on the porch with the cell-phone.)*

(BELEN *lies on the sofa.*)

(ADORACIÓN *lurks.*)

VANESSA: Cheo...it's me again...I thought you'd call after the meeting. A day ago! Don't know if you're in jail or what. Belen's in bad shape. I dragged her out of bed. She's on the sofa away from the ghost. *(Whispers)* I saw her. *The ghost girl.* I'm highly freaked...but I wanna talk to her...God, I'm losing my mind! Call immediately. I will put aside my outrage the second I hear your voice.

(VANESSA *turns off the phone.*)

(ISMAEL *approaches.*)

ISMAEL: Vanessa?

(VANESSA *turns, regards him with contempt.*)

VANESSA: I'll break your face for what you did.

ISMAEL: *I think you need to turn on your television.*

VANESSA: Why?

(ISMAEL *goes into* BELEN'*s house, turns on the T V. A voice on the T V reads off names.*)

(VANESSA *watches in silence.*)

ISMAEL: *They say there was an F B I informant among the New Nationalists...when the leaders from all the independence parties showed up...soldiers surrounded the house. There were negotiations, a stand off. Then the shooting. They're calling it "Massacre in Arecibo."* (*Indicating the T V*) *They're showing the names of the dead...*

VANESSA: (*After a few moments*) ...Kevin Alejandro Betances...

ISMAEL: *I thought he was wasting his time, pushing us into a disaster...but I never wanted this. We grew up side-by-side, you know. We used to swim in La Posa together.*

(*Beat.* VANESSA *is too numb to move or speak.*)

ISMAEL: *I'll stay or go, whatever you want.*

VANESSA: (*Barely audible*) Go, Izzy.

ISMAEL: (*After a beat*) *God Almighty. What are we doing?* (*He leaves.*)

(VANESSA, *alone, devastated, watches T V.*)

Scene Six

(*Three days later. Afternoon*)

(BELEN, *dressed in black, enters supported by* ISMAEL *wearing a black jacket.*)

BELEN: In the past...no matter how bad things got... Puerto Ricans were allowed to die in privacy. I've never seen police at a funeral before, Ismael, television cameras.

ISMAEL: The police are there to keep the peace.

BELEN: The same motherfuckers who shot him—?

ISMAEL: Nobody knows who shot who—

BELEN: It's a sin to bring a rifle to a funeral. Says so somewhere in Genesis.

ISMAEL: *(Has said it before)* When they buried the other independence leaders, there was violence. I think the gringos—

BELEN: The gringos have finished this island, Ismael! They took away a saint of a boy and they will take more and more until all that's left are the robots and degenerates and collaborators!

ISMAEL: *(Admiring her grit)* Seems like you're feeling better...

BELEN: Something's been awakened. I don't like how it feels. The way people look at you.

ISMAEL: We can't go back to being asleep.

BELEN: This is an *island*, Ismael. It floats on the ocean like a cloud. It's made for loving and dreaming, and spending time with God and when death happened there was never this kind of rage.

ISMAEL: That was a long time ago, before we were born.

BELEN: You're an imbecile but I still love you like a son.

ISMAEL: *(Teasing her)* You're much too kind, Doña Belen.

(VANESSA *enters. She wears black. She crosses to* ISMAEL.)

VANESSA: Thanks for walking her home, Izzy.

ISMAEL: *I didn't want to say this at the funeral, there was enough tension, but friends from Las Arenas, who grew up with Kevin—I mean Cheo—we're thinking of holding a vigil for him, here, in two weeks. Completely nonviolent, nonpartisan, just a remembrance of the man. And I hope you can be there too. And Doña Belen of course. (Beat) And*

when it's over, I promise I'll do everything to make sure the
actions of the police and F B I are investigated. Hear me?
Then we'll see how good this gringo justice really is.

VANESSA: *(Appreciatively)* Maybe I'll say a few words at
the vigil.

ISMAEL: *(To* BELEN, *re* VANESSA*)* Boricua flower.

VANESSA: But I want to do it in Spanish, so you'll have
to help me with the translation.

ISMAEL: *(Pleased) Of course. If you need anything else, I'm*
the house with the Puero Rican flag on the second floor.

(ISMAEL *goes to* BELEN, *kisses her.)*

BELEN: May the Everlasting Love of Christ be in the
food you eat, the water that bathes you, and in the eyes
and words of everyone who loves you. Amen.

ISMAEL: Sleep in peace. *(He leaves the house.)*

(BELEN *watches* VANESSA *a moment.)*

BELEN: *(Mimes drinking)* Water?

VANESSA: *Rum.*

BELEN: Yeah, okay.

(VANESSA *gets a bottle of rum.)*

BELEN: Toli and I used to make this shit at home...I
don't have the energy to make it anymore...but I buy it
by the bathtub-full.

(BELEN *hands* VANESSA *a shot glass.)*

(VANESSA *downs it.)*

(VANESSA's *Spanish, though vastly improved, is still*
strongly accented and halting.)

VANESSA: *More. Please.*

(BELEN *gives* VANESSA *another.)*

BELEN: *(After a beat) Good morning, Teacher.*

VANESSA: *Good morning, little-grandma.*

BELEN: *How are you, angel?*

VANESSA: *Sad today.*

BELEN: I know you loved him. I was so happy to see the two of you together.

VANESSA: *I think...my heart...is killing me in pain. No eyes Cheo, no ears—no touch him. He is never.*

BELEN: Only his body is gone, dear. Only. His Body. Is gone.

VANESSA: *The body...it was...his hands, his kissings...his body was mine. Now it is the earth. All dead, he dead...all lost, he dead...all nothing, he dead. I wish God be dead...!*

BELEN: No my love, don't say—

VANESSA: *Yes! God is to crucify me. God is to hurt me...to make His skyhome...*

BELEN: Heaven.

VANESSA: *He make Heaven happy for God...but hurt girl who loving Cheo. It's all full of shit!*

BELEN: Full of shit? Who taught you full of shit?

VANESSA: *(Almost smiles) Cheo teach me...shit, cunt, bitch, asshole, whore, pimp, pussy, dick, tits, blowjob, I shit on God, I shit on your mother, I shit on the President, I—*

BELEN: Okay, you can stop now, I didn't know Cheo was such a good teacher.

VANESSA: *I was almost laughing...Cheo's, how you say it? Hole, earth.*

BELEN: Grave.

VANESSA: *Cheo's grave...at end, at the far end—*

BELEN: At the edge.

VANESSA: *Cheo's grave at the edge of the cemetery. The fence. Other side, the little—*

BELEN: The little farm.

VANESSA: *The little farm. The cow and the horses...to the fence...to watch Cheo, to cover dirt.*

BELEN: Being buried.

VANESSA: *A cow and two horses go—*

BELEN: Went.

VANESSA: *Went to the fence to watch Cheo being buried. Silent, and they is to is—big eyes! Their big eyes went watching us being buried Cheo.*

BELEN: They knew. They looked sympathetically at us, dear angel, and they came to say goodbye. I wonder if animals feel pity for us when they see us bury our children. If I were an animal or an angel I'd feel sorry for the pathetic death of men and women. Of all the animals in the world we're the only ones who don't know how to let go.

VANESSA: You were so beautiful today. God, I watched you during that funeral and I swear I could feel the earth spinning under me. I learned about birth and death and war and power by studying the lines on your face.

BELEN: We old women know how to do funerals. I'm going to make us some food.

VANESSA: *I'm not hungry.*

BELEN: You're going to eat this. I can make you eat.

VANESSA: *Okay, but I can make the food. You sick. You rest.*

BELEN: I don't feel sick today. I want to cook for you and take care of you, may the Infinite Love of...oh, Christ, I'm too tired to come up with a good blessing right now.

(VANESSA's *cellphone rings.*)

(BELEN *kisses* VANESSA, *then goes to the offstage kitchen.*)

VANESSA: *(On phone)* Hi Mami. *(Beat)* It was this morning. *(Beat)* Fine but I'm more tired than I can explain. How's Papi? *(Beat)* Tell him hi, okay? And I love him. And I want him to be well. *(Beat)* I'm going to stay. I'm not going back to Paterson and all the madness. I'm going to apply to the University of Puerto Rico at Rio Piedras. Soon as they re-open it. *(Beat)* I know it's dangerous! Don't make me curse you on the day I buried my boyfriend, okay? *(Beat)* Then come down here and get me, Ma'! See this place for yourself! You know, you tell stories and play the music and get all weepy, but you're never here! And your Spanish is atrocious! So come here, stay here a little, and then we'll talk. Got it, *Florencia? (She turns off the phone. She walks to the bed and collapses.)*

(ADORACIÓN *gets into bed with* VANESSA.*)*

(BELEN *watches* VANESSA *lie in bed.* BELEN *decides to let her stay.* BELEN *goes out to the porch, lights up a cigarette, looks up at the stars, thinks.)*

ADORACIÓN: *(To* VANESSA*)* The old lady, she lied to you. Yes, I slept with Don Toli and everyone in Las Arenas knew—including Doña Belen. But no one dared say a word. Then I got pregnant. And that changed everything. He stopped wanting me—completely. I was so desperate, one day I went to church to look for him. He was there—next to Belen. She looked at my growing belly, her mouth opened for one word: *whore.* Over and over—in front of God, Mary, the entire town. Soon I was known at the Mulatta Whore of Las Arenas. When Don Toli started saying it too—the words were like knives right into my body! My baby was born...and the dirty words of Las Arenas killed me. The day I was buried, Don Toli came to my house and my mother gave him my baby. And he took my baby to Belen and said, "This is our baby now. Celia is *our* baby." Belen said yes. And took her in. And never told you that your grandmother Celia was my baby. *(In English) Vanessa—you my baby.*

(VANESSA *looks at her, understanding but not being able to reply.)*

ADORACIÓN: Ay! It was what the old witch wanted more than anything, to make life, to see it coming out from between her legs, complete, breathing, hearing it laugh, its little fingers scrambling up to touch her. She never had that. All her stillborn hopes are buried under a Ceiba tree in Las Arenas. Each branch of the tree is another dead hope. My one baby—my girl—walked away from all that death. To think, to pray—and maybe, somehow, if there's justice, to remember the passage from my body into the humid air. To remember the liquid I surrounded her with, the thunder of my heart, the salt sea-water of my blood. I told you to live and you did...

(ADORACIÓN *kisses* VANESSA, *who kisses and holds her.)*

(VANESSA *gets out of bed.)*

(ADORACIÓN *gets out of bed.)*

(VANESSA *goes to the porch, to* BELEN, *sitting on the rocking chair.)*

(BELEN *doesn't have to look at* VANESSA *to know what happened.)*

VANESSA: *Is she my great-grandmother?*

(BELEN *starts to cry, a cry she can't control, a cry that seems to break her body in half.)*

(ADORACIÓN *watches.)*

(VANESSA *goes to* BELEN *and holds her.)*

VANESSA: *Little-grandma...it's okay...*

(BELEN *wipes her eyes, and looks at* ADORACIÓN.)

BELEN: I'm the last of my kind, Vanessa. There's nobody like me in the whole world. What I carry in my skin. What I know of life. What I remember of this island. But I'm as fertile as a stone. I have nothing to pass on but a haunted bed, a couple of poems they wrote about me, but I don't know where they are. I wanted so much to see my mother in your smile. To hear my sisters on your tongue. *(She looks at* ADORACIÓN. *Her words are as much for* ADORACIÓN *as they are for* VANESSA.*)* Oh, my dear...now I think I know the pain I made old Toli feel when I didn't forgive him. The pain I made your great-grandmother feel. The worst pain—the pain of extinction...

ADORACIÓN: Yes. *(She starts to leave the house.)*

(BELEN *gets up from her chair. Faces* ADORACIÓN.*)*

BELEN: Adoración Celia Lomar!

(ADORACIÓN *stops and looks at* BELEN.*)*

BELEN: I am sorry I took your daughter and killed you with my words. That was unkind of me.

ADORACIÓN: *(Admiring her honesty)* Ay, Belen...

(ADORACIÓN *approaches* BELEN.*)*

BELEN: Tell Toli that I'm sorry and that I understand something I didn't understand before. I understand why he loved you.

(ADORACIÓN *embraces* BELEN. *The old adversaries hold each other. Touching* ADORACIÓN *gives* BELEN *new energy and resolve.)*

ADORACIÓN: Do you want to tell him yourself?

BELEN: Is he near?

ADORACIÓN: Just beyond those trees. Come with me.

(BELEN *thinks about the implications. Looks around at the world she's known for over a century.)*

BELEN: It's not mine anymore, this old island.

ADORACIÓN: Are you ready, then?

(BELEN *nods yes and goes to* VANESSA, *who's been watching this scene with some awe and sadness.* BELEN *embraces her.*)

BELEN: I'm going with my friend now.

VANESSA: *Are you sure?*

BELEN: I'm between a hundred and a hundred and fifty years old. It's time.

VANESSA: *I'll miss you, little grand-ma.*

BELEN: Is that the best you can do? Have I taught you nothing?

(VANESSA *touches* BELEN's *ancient face and tries not to cry.*)

VANESSA: May you find a wild heaven full of love...and a God that'll plant joy in your wounded heart, dear, adored Doña Belen.

BELEN: Better.

(*They kiss and* BELEN *goes back to* ADORACIÓN. *The women embrace and leave the house together...and disappear into the forest in silence.*)

(VANESSA *is alone now. The house is hers.*)

(VANESSA *goes into the house...goes into the bedroom...looks at the bed...and gets an idea.*)

(*Lights change. It becomes night.*)

(VANESSA *calls out to the universe.*)

VANESSA: (*Imitating* BELEN) Kevin Alejandro Betances! (*She gets into bed and waits.*)

(CHEO *appears. He looks at* VANESSA, *unsure.*)

(VANESSA *looks at him, smiles, and taps the side of the bed next to her.*)

(CHEO's *melancholy smile...he gets into bed with her.*)

(*Lights begin to go down.*)

(*The young lovers hold each other.*)

(VANESSA *and* CHEO *fall asleep together in* BELEN's *magic bed as the sound of coquis begins and fills the stage.*)

(*Black out*)

END OF PLAY

www.ingramcontent.com/pod-product-compliance
Lightning Source LLC
Chambersburg PA
CBHW052220090426
42741CB00010B/2614